How do I feel about

WHEN PEOPLE DIE

Sarah Levete

COPPER BEECH BOOKS • BROOKFIELD, CONNECTICUT

Designed and produced by
Aladdin Books Ltd
28 Percy Street
London W1P 0LD

First published in the United States
in 1998 by
Copper Beech Books,
an imprint of
The Millbrook Press
2 Old New Milford Road
Brookfield, Connecticut 06804

Printed in Duabi
5 4 3

Designer   Gary Edgar-Hyde
Editor   Jen Green
Illustrator   Christopher O'Neill
Photographer   Roger Vlitos

Library of Congress
Cataloging-in-Publication Data
Levete, Sarah.
When people die / Sarah Levete ; illustrated by
Christopher O'Neill.
p. cm. — (How do I feel about)
Includes index.
Summary: Describes how people feel about death,
discussing what happens when someone dies, why
people die, and how to cope with grief.
ISBN 0-7613-0870-9 (lib. bdg.)
1. Children and death—Juvenile literature.
2. Bereavement in children—Juvenile literature.
3. Grief in children—Juvenile literature.
[1. Death. 2. Grief.] I. O'Neill, Christopher, ill.
II. Title. III. Series.
BF723.D3L444 1998   98-16959
155.9'37—dc21   CIP AC

Contents

Introduction

Kate, Ben, Ima, Annie, and Matt are all friends. They have all known someone who has died. Each of them had different feelings and reactions. There is lots of fear and mystery about death, though it is a natural part of life. Join the friends as they discuss how they felt and how they coped when someone died.

Dying is as natural as being born.

If a friend is upset by a death, you can try to help comfort him or her.

When someone dies you have lots of confusing feelings.

Getting over the death of someone you love takes time.

People die for lots of different reasons.

BEN

KATE

ANNIE

IMA

MATT

What Is Dying?

Matt is showing Ben a photo of his cat, Buttons, who died over the weekend. Matt feels very sad and really misses Buttons. But he knows that every living thing must die some time. Buttons' body was not well enough to carry on living. Death is when the body stops working. People and animals are born, they live their lives, and then they die.

People are born.

People grow old.

▼ Death Is Natural

If you look around your house or yard, you will see lots of living things. Each has been born and will die one day. Even a tree, which has lived for hundreds of years, may be blown down in a very strong wind and die.

◄ No Longer Working

When a person dies, his or her body stops working, like a toy that can't be fixed. A toy no longer works because it is worn out. In the same way, a person may die because his or her body is too old to work anymore.

Matt, tell us about Buttons.

"I feel really sad about Buttons dying. I miss her so much, but she was very old and her body was worn out. I know we couldn't have done anything more to help her. Mom says that dying is the most natural thing in the world. Everything that lives has to die — it's just how nature works."

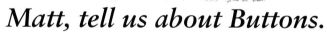

Why Do People Die?

Kate recently joined Ima's class at school. Kate is telling Ima that her best friend, Eva, died from an illness. The doctors couldn't make her better. Ima's uncle was killed in an accident two years ago. There are many reasons why people die. They may be ill or very old, or death may be caused by an accident.

Bodies get tired. Finally, the body dies.

Accidents cause injury and even death.

▶ *Illness*

Sometimes you feel ill. In time your body heals itself, or you take medicine to make yourself feel better. But even medicine can't make some people well again — they may be too ill to get better.

This will soon make you feel better.

◀ *Old Age*

Even after a long, healthy, and happy life, the body will get tired. In the end it will just stop working.

But whatever the cause of death, people who were close to the person who has died will often feel very sad.

I can't run like I used to.

▼ *Accidents*

Death can come without warning to healthy people. People may die in an accident, such as a car crash. Or they may die in a disaster, such as a flood. An accident can happen to a person who is young or old.

Two people died in a train crash...

Why Do People Die?

1. When Bill's sister, Amy, was born, she wasn't very well.

"Come on, Amy, let's go outside."

"Amy must have her medicine first."

"She needs the medicine to make her well."

2. The doctors tried giving her different medicines to make her better.

3. Amy died when she was three. Her body wasn't well enough to stay alive.

Why did Amy die?

Amy was ill for a long time. She didn't die suddenly. Her body slowly stopped working. The doctors tried to make Amy better but the different medicines didn't work.

Sometimes people die very quickly. But it can take quite a long time, as it did for Amy.

8

▼ Gone to Sleep?

Some grown-ups think it is better if young people don't understand about death. They may say that someone who has died has "gone to sleep" or "gone away." But death is not like sleep or going away, because the dead person will not wake up or come back. It is often better to be told the truth.

◄ Don't Feel Guilty

You may feel worried or guilty if you said something rude or were mean to someone before he or she died. But you are not to blame. A person only dies because his or her body stops working.

Did Grandpa die because I didn't want him to stay at our house?

But if he's gone away he'll come back.

Ima, why did your uncle die?

"My uncle died in a car accident. He was only forty. It seems so unfair. I used to think it was just old people who died, but it's not. Mom told me he had gone away, so I kept waiting for him to come back. But I knew something was wrong. In the end mom told me the truth. I still felt sad, but at least I understood."

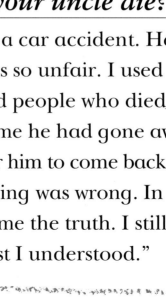

What Happens After Death?

At school, Kate and Annie are doing a project on different ideas about death. Nobody knows for sure what happens after death, but lots of people have strong beliefs. Whatever your beliefs, there are funerals and other ways that let you say a special goodbye to a person who has died. There are different kinds of burial as well.

What do you think happens when you die?

I think you have a spirit that lives on after your body dies.

Some people's bodies are buried…

…others are burned, or cremated.

▼ Saying Goodbye

Funerals and other customs can help you say goodbye to someone who has died.

The body may be buried in the ground or cremated — burned in a very hot fire. The ashes may be put in a place the person loved. Whatever happens to the body after death, it doesn't hurt — the body cannot feel anything.

I believe that souls go to heaven.

I believe that a person is reborn in another body.

◀ Different Ideas

People have different beliefs about death. Some believe that everyone has a soul or spirit, which lives on when the body dies. Others believe that a person who has died is reborn as another person or animal. Some people think that a person who has died continues to live on in our memories.

Kate, how did you feel about going to Eva's funeral?

"Mom and Dad didn't want me to go to the funeral at first. I knew the funeral would be very sad, but I wanted to go and say goodbye to Eva properly. I talked it over with Mom and Dad, and in the end they let me go."

What Happens When Someone Dies?

Ima and Annie have been talking about how people feel when someone dies. Everyone reacts differently to a death. A person's reaction depends on many things, such as how close they were to the dead person. Some people cry a lot. Others think it's better not to cry. Annie's brother Joe died recently in a motorcycle accident. Annie's mom found it hard to accept what had happened.

Your brother's death was so sudden.

My mom still finds it hard to believe.

Crying helps express how you feel.

Some people try to hide their feelings.

▼ In Shock

If someone dies very suddenly, relatives and friends may go into shock. They may feel numb, and find it difficult to believe what has happened. They may find it hard to eat or sleep.

Other people don't feel much right away. Their feelings may come out later.

your grandpa had a long and happy life.

◀ Sudden or Expected

Some deaths are unexpected. Relatives and friends may feel upset they didn't say goodbye. Some deaths are more expected, because the person who has died was old or ill. A death that is expected may be easier to cope with than a sudden death.

I'm sorry, but I can't eat anything.

Annie, how did your family react to Joe's death?

"Everyone reacted differently. Dad was very practical and organized everything for the funeral. Mom was in shock. I felt really upset, but didn't want to make things worse, so I tried not to show my feelings. At the funeral we all cried a lot and I felt a bit better afterward."

How Do You Feel?

Matt is over at Kate's house, talking about Eva. Kate says she still feels upset about Eva's death. When someone dies, you may feel sad and miserable. You may feel angry. You may feel all of these, or just confused. These feelings are all part of a natural process called grieving. This is part of getting over someone's death.

How long has it taken you to feel better since Eva died?

I still feel sad sometimes. I think I'll always miss Eva.

You may feel very lonely.

You may find it hard to sleep at first.

How Do You Feel?

▼ Feeling Angry

At first you may feel angry with the person who has died for leaving you. You may feel he or she has let you down. Or you may feel angry with the person who has died for making other people sad. It's not unusual to feel angry when someone dies.

I just can't concentrate.

I hate Mom for leaving us.

▶ Talking Helps

Whether you feel sad, upset, or angry, talking about it will help. Don't bottle up your feelings inside. Try to tell a grown-up or a good friend how you feel.

It won't make the sad or difficult feelings go away, but it can help you to feel better.

◀ At School

If you are sad because someone has died, you may find it hard to concentrate at school. Feeling upset can make you behave badly and get into trouble. But taking out your unhappy feelings on others won't help.

Talk to a teacher you trust and explain what has happened.

Thanks. I feel a bit better now.

1. Sean's mom died a month ago. Sean didn't want his dad to go to work.

2. Sean felt too scared to sleep at night. He went downstairs to see his dad.

3. Sean's dad explained that he wasn't going to die and leave Sean too.

Why was Sean scared?

Sean's mom had died when she was young. Sean was frightened that his dad might die as well.

It is quite natural to feel scared if a parent or guardian dies. If you are worried about who will look after you, talk about your worries to a grown-up who is close to you.

▼ Feeling Confused

It can be difficult to see people upset at the death of a person they argued with. But people do argue, even when they love each other. Even if you didn't get along well with someone who died, your actions had nothing to do with the death.

It's not fair. Why was it my mom who died?

◄ It's Not Fair

It can seem unfair when someone close to you dies, especially if he or she was not old. You may feel angry that it was not someone else who died instead. But wishing it had happened to someone else will not help. Explain how you feel to someone you trust.

Matt, how did you feel when your grandmother died?

"At first I didn't really feel very much when Grandma died. I cried more when Buttons died than when Grandma died. But that didn't mean I didn't love Grandma. Now, when we go to the park where Grandma used to take us, I really miss her."

17

Learning To Cope

Ben persuaded Kate to join in a ball game. Kate told Ben that after Eva's death she didn't want to play with other friends. But Kate's mom told her that she could still remember Eva even if she was enjoying herself. If someone dies, you will have lots of different feelings. You will start feeling better, although it may take a long time.

One minute you may feel sad.

18

The next minute you may feel OK.

▼ Show Your Feelings

If someone close to you has died, you may have lots of difficult feelings, including anger, sadness, and loneliness.

Don't hide your feelings. It may help to make a model out of clay, or paint a picture to show how you feel.

▶ Special Occasions

Birthdays and other special occasions can make you feel very sad. If you miss the person who has died, you could draw them a picture or write them a letter.

You may also find that it helps to talk in your head to the person who has died.

◀ Feeling Better

Just because someone has died, it doesn't mean that you have to forget him or her, or stop loving them. It may take time, but you will feel better. You will be able to enjoy life again, and also remember the good times you shared with the person who has died.

1. Isha's sister died in an accident. Isha felt sad and guilty at the same time.

Bella was such a good girl. I still miss her so much.

2. One day Isha heard her mom and dad saying how good Bella always was.

But Bella was naughty sometimes, too. Don't they love me?

3. Later Isha told her best friend, Ali, about what she had heard.

What can Isha do?

Isha should talk to her parents about how she feels. When someone dies, people often remember just the good things. Of course Isha's parents miss Bella, but that doesn't mean that they don't love Isha. If you feel miserable and left out because someone has died, try talking about your feelings with a grown-up who you trust.

▼ Moving On

If someone who was close to you has died, you may feel that you shouldn't enjoy yourself. You may feel guilty about having fun. But you can still have strong feelings for the person who has died, and live your life fully.

It's OK to feel happy and make new friends.

◀ Show You Care

If you know someone whose friend or relative has died, try to imagine how he or she must be feeling. Make a special effort to be understanding and caring toward that person.

You can help by making sure they don't feel left out.

Ben, how should you behave toward someone who is grieving?

"There's no right or wrong way to behave. My best friend is Jim. His dad died last year. At first I didn't know what to say to him. I felt uncomfortable. Mom said to be myself but be kind. If you know someone who has lost a friend or relative, you can help by showing you care."

21

Don't Forget...

Kate, did you ever feel confused when Eva died?

"I felt lots of different things when Eva died. It was really confusing, but it helped me to talk to my parents about it. Sometimes now when I feel sad it can help me feel better if I draw a picture."

Matt, do you still think about Buttons?

"If a person or animal you love dies, you will feel very sad. After a while, you stop feeling quite so sad. But that doesn't mean that you forget the person or animal. I've got a new cat, Poppy, now. I really like her, but I still miss Buttons. I think about my grandma now more than I did when she first died. I remember the good times we had."

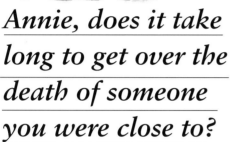

Annie, does it take long to get over the death of someone you were close to?

"Getting over the death of a friend or relative may take a long time. To begin with you may not want to play with friends. But in the end, you will feel better and have good memories about happy times you shared with the person who has died."

Ima and Ben, how can you help if you know someone whose friend or relative has died?

"If you know someone who is grieving, be especially kind to him or her. It can make a big difference if you show you care, even if your friend isn't ready to play or to have fun yet. When you are unhappy, friends can really help to make you feel better."

23

Index

All the photographs in this book have been posed by models. The publishers would like to thank them all.